A Rose Named Peace

HOW
FRANCIS MEILLAND
CREATED
A FLOWER OF HOPE
FOR A WORLD AT WAR

Barbara Carroll Roberts

illustrated by Bagram Ibatoulline

CANDLEWICK PRESS

Once there was a boy who loved roses.
Fat rosebuds unfurling under the warm summer sun.
Petals, soft as lambs' ears, between his fingers. Perfume,
light and sweet, floating on the breeze.

The boy's name was Francis Meilland.

He was born in 1912 on his family's farm in southern France, where they grew fruit trees, vegetables, and roses. They sold their fruit and vegetables at the village market.

And their roses—they sold their roses to gardeners all over Europe, packaging the small plants with care, sending them out to grow and bloom in far-off gardens.

Francis always knew he wanted to be a rose grower, like his father and his grandfathers. On days when he didn't have school, instead of playing with friends, he worked beside his father, watching closely, learning the skills he'd need to grow his own roses one day.

When Francis was seventeen, he and his father visited a rose grower in a neighboring town. Strolling through the man's garden, Francis stopped to gaze at a rose unlike any he'd seen before. A rosebush covered in yellow blooms, golden sunbursts with forty petals on each flower. What was it?

A brand-new rose, the gardener explained. He had created it by cross-pollinating two other rosebushes.

Francis bent low over the flowers in wonder.

What would it be like to create a new rose? A new thing of beauty to give to the world?

As soon as he got home, Francis raced to his family's rose beds, combing through the long rows, noting the sturdiness of one bush, the glossy green leaves of another, the velvety crimson of this flower, the flaming orange-red of that one.

Finally he selected two rosebushes to cross-pollinate, to create his first new rose.

At dawn the next morning, before the sun could warm the buds and coax them open, Francis peeled back the petals from the two roses he'd chosen and sprinkled pollen from the flowers of one bush onto the flowers of the other.

And then he waited.

He waited through the summer until the rose hips—the fruit of the rose plant—swelled and ripened in the fall. Francis harvested the rose hips, cut them open, removed the seeds, and planted them.

Then he waited again.

He waited for the seeds to sprout and grow into new rosebushes. Then waited for the new plants to bloom, to see if one of these new roses would be more beautiful than any of the others his family grew.

But they weren't.

The next year, Francis tried again. And again and again in the years that followed. Making thousands of different crosses, keeping careful records in his notebooks, studying the new plants as they pushed up through the soil, tending them with care, always striving to create a rose more beautiful than any seen before.

But so many things went wrong.

Sudden frosts killed fragile seedlings. Mildew and insects destroyed rows and rows of plants. Even Caddy, the family's dog, damaged the new roses by tearing up an entire planting bed to bury her bone.

And there was always so much waiting.

Waiting for each new hybrid to grow and bloom through several seasons before Francis could be sure of the sturdiness of the plant, the quality of the flower.

There were days when he wanted to give up.

Yet slowly, slowly, he began to have success. He sent a few promising new roses to growers in other countries to be tested in different soils and different climates.

A rose grower in the United States, Robert Pyle, loved the new roses Francis sent to him. They flourished in his nursery. He offered to sell Meilland roses in America.

Francis agreed, happy that so many more people would soon enjoy the beauty of his roses.

One June day in 1939, Francis invited rose growers from many countries to spend a day at his family's farm, to see all the new roses he had created.

And just as Francis had done in his neighbor's garden when he was seventeen, his guests stopped and stared at one rose. An enormous rose—five inches across in full bloom—with petals that shaded from pale ivory at the center through creamy yellow to a fringe of deep pink at their outer edges.

No one had ever seen a rose like it.

The new rose was called 3-35-40, meaning it was the third cross Francis had made in 1935 and the fortieth plant that had grown from the seeds of that cross.

Francis promised his friends he would send them cuttings of 3-35-40 to test in their own gardens.

Then catastrophe struck.
Not just for the Meillands.
For the world.
In September 1939, the German army marched into
Poland, and World War II exploded across Europe.

As quickly as he could, Francis packaged up cuttings of 3-35-40 and sent them to rose growers he knew in Germany and Italy and to Robert Pyle in the United States.

Now French soldiers needed food, and because they could not eat roses, Francis and his father dug up almost all of their roses—twenty thousand rosebushes on acres and acres of land.

And burned them.

Except for one tiny patch of ground where Francis kept a few
rosebushes, the Meillands would grow only vegetables on their farm.

When the German army invaded France, postal service between France and other countries stopped, so Francis had no way to contact his rose-growing friends.

What had happened to the packages of 3-35-40? Had they reached the other growers? Or had they been lost and destroyed in the war?

Years went by, and all across Europe, across Asia, North Africa, even on tiny islands in the Pacific Ocean, the most terrible war the world had ever seen raged on. Whole cities destroyed by bombs. Farms and forests blasted to dust. Families torn apart and scattered. Millions of people left starving, homeless. Tens of millions of people killed.

But the Meillands' farm in southern France was spared. No battles blazed across its orchards. No armies trampled its fields. Francis and his family continued growing vegetables.

And when he could, Francis tended his small bed of roses, giving them the care they needed to thrive and bloom every spring, a tiny island of peace and beauty amid the terrors of war.

Finally, at the end of April 1945, the Allied armies swept into Berlin, Germany's capital, and the German army surrendered.

The war in Europe was over at last.
Francis rejoiced with his family. With his neighbors.
With people all around the world.

A few months later, a letter arrived from the United States, one of the first letters to reach Francis since the war had begun. It was from Robert Pyle.

He had received the packet of 3-35-40 in 1939, Robert said, and the rose had thrived in his planting beds in Pennsylvania. He'd sent cuttings to friends in the American Midwest, with its freezing winters and humid summers, to growers in the deserts of the Southwest, to others in rain-drenched Oregon, and to still others in California.

And everywhere, the rose grew vigorously and
bloomed out full with its pink-tipped golden flowers.

Robert knew that people all around the world would want to plant this rose in their gardens. But it needed a name. And so, because he had not been able to ask Francis what to name the rose, Robert had chosen a name he hoped Francis would agree captured the essence of its beauty.

On April 29, 1945, just as the German army was surrendering in Berlin, Robert had presented the new rose at a ceremony in California. And as two white doves soared up into the sky, Robert said, "We are persuaded that this greatest new rose of our time should be named for the world's greatest desire: Peace."

Francis read Robert's letter again and again. His rose, a rose that had survived a terrible war, was now so much more than just a beautiful flower.

Now, when people watched its fat rosebuds unfurl beneath the warm summer sun; when they touched its petals, soft as lambs' ears, between their fingers; when they breathed in its sweet, light scent and gazed at the glory of its flowers in full bloom, they would see hope for peace in every corner of the world.

AFTERWORD

Francis Meilland continued growing roses after World War II, creating many more beautiful new varieties, but he always referred to the Peace rose as his masterpiece.

What pride one feels, and what a reward for a gardener to know that his rose is growing everywhere, in little gardens, in great parks, around churches, temples, mosques, and hospitals. . . . How strange it is to remember also that these millions of roses, without exception, have all come from a single seed no larger than the head of a pin.

—Francis Meilland

Today, rose experts estimate that there are more than one hundred million Peace rosebushes blooming all around the world.

Perhaps one day you'll plant a Peace rose in your garden, too.

THE NAME OF A ROSE

Because communications between people in different countries were stopped during World War II, Francis Meilland and the rose growers to whom he sent the cuttings of 3-35-40 couldn't tell one another what they were doing. In 1942, Francis named the rose after his mother, Madame Antoine Meilland. In Germany, the rose grower who received the cuttings named the rose Gloria Dei—"Glory to God." In Italy, the rose grower named it Gioia—"Joy."

In these countries, 3-35-40 is still known by these names, but throughout the rest of the world, this beautiful rose is called Peace.

A PLANT PATENT

In the 1940s, the United States was one of the only countries that allowed gardeners to patent new varieties of roses and other plants that they created. A patent meant that if anyone else sold that plant to other people, the seller had to pay a small amount of the sale price to the plant's creator.

When Robert Pyle introduced the Peace rose in the United States in 1945, he had no idea if Francis Meilland had survived the war. Still, Robert filed a US patent in Francis's name. The money that came to Francis from that patent allowed him to rebuild his family's rose business after World War II.

GROWING MORE ROSES

The cuttings of the Peace rose that Francis sent to Robert Pyle and the other rose growers were small sections of the branches of a rosebush. The growers grafted, or attached, the cuttings to rootstock, the roots of another rosebush from which the branches had been removed. Soon new shoots, leaves, and flowers grew from the cuttings. The growers then repeated the process, taking more cuttings, grafting them to more rootstock, growing more and more Peace rosebushes. This method of plant propagation is used for many kinds of bushes and trees.

MEILLAND ROSES

Francis Meilland followed in the footsteps of his father and grandfathers, growing roses on their farm in southern France. Francis's children continued the family rose business. Today, Meilland roses are still grown—and shipped all over the world—by Francis's grandchildren.

GLOSSARY

ANTHER – The top part of a flower's stamen, where pollen is produced

CROSS-POLLINATE – To transfer the pollen from the anthers of a flower on one plant to the stigma of a flower on another plant. Bees, insects, and even the wind cross-pollinate plants in nature. Usually this natural cross-pollination occurs between plants of the same variety, as when bees cross-pollinate the fruit trees in an orchard. People can also cross-pollinate plants to create desired hybrids.

HYBRID – A plant that is a cross between two different varieties of a plant

PISTIL – The female part of a flower, consisting of the stigma, style, and ovary

POLLEN – The powdery grains produced by the male part of a flower, which pollinate the female part of the flower, causing it to produce seeds

STAMEN – The male part of a flower, consisting of the filament and the anther

STIGMA – The top of the female part of a flower, which collects the pollen released from the anthers

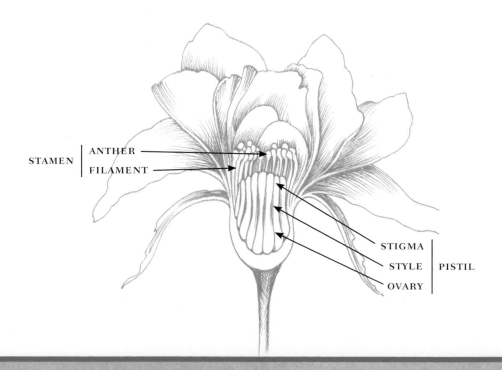

BIBLIOGRAPHY

The author is grateful to Matthias Meilland for his assistance in researching this book. The following resources were also instructive:

Conard-Pyle Company Records. MSS 634. Special Collections. University of Delaware Library, Newark.

Harkness, Jack. *The Makers of Heavenly Roses.* London: Souvenir Press, 1985.

Meilland, Alain, and Gilles Lambert. *Meilland: A Life in Roses.* Translated by Richard C. Keating and L. Clark Keating. Carbondale: Southern Illinois University Press, 1984. Originally published as *La Vie en Roses* (Paris: Éditions Solar, 1969).

Meilland, Francis. "My Masterpiece." *The Rose Annual,* 1953, 110–114.

Miller, Donald L. *The Story of World War II.* Revised, expanded, and updated from the original text by Henry Steele Commager. New York: Simon and Schuster, 2001.

Ridge, Antonia. *For Love of a Rose.* London: Faber and Faber, 1965.

In memory of my neighbor and fellow gardener
Laura Hoffman, who first told me a small part of this story;

For my friend and fellow nonfiction writer Patricia Sutton,
who told me to do more research and make this story into a book;

And for the Meilland family, who continue to send the beauty —
as well as the Joy, Glory, and Peace — of their roses out into the world.

BCR

To my friend Tatiana Aleksa,
the passionate gardener

BI

First edition 2022

Library of Congress Catalog Card Number pending
ISBN 978-1-5362-0843-6

22 23 24 25 26 27 TLF 10 9 8 7 6 5 4 3 2 1

Printed in Dongguan, Guangdong, China

This book was typeset in Fairfield LH.
The illustrations were done in watercolor.

Candlewick Press
99 Dover Street
Somerville, Massachusetts 02144

www.candlewick.com